Traveler for God

A story about John Neumann

written by Dolores Ready
illustrated by Constance Crawford

© 1977 by Winston Press, Inc.
printed in the United States of America
all rights reserved

ISBN: 0-03-022111-0
Library of Congress Catalog Card Number: 77-077679

 Winston Press 430 Oak Grove Minneapolis, MN 55403

"Get below!" The ship's captain shouted at the
small man standing on the deck. The wind howled.
A terrible storm was blowing up. "Get below!"
But John Neumann did not hear the captain.
The storm made too much noise.

John stood and watched the ocean leap at
the ship. He had never seen a storm at sea.
He had only seen storms over the mountains and
forests and villages of Bohemia. (Bohemia was a
country far away across the Atlantic Ocean.
The people there spoke German.) Already John was
missing his home in Bohemia. His mother and father
and sisters and brother were far away from him now.
Maybe he would never see them again. And all
because he thought he was needed in America.
Maybe he should not be making this long journey.

The wind howled more fiercely than ever. The sea sprang onto the deck of the ship and soaked John's clothes. Suddenly, John felt the urge to move away from where he was standing. He jumped aside quickly. And just in time, too. For the wind had cracked a mast. It fell to the deck right where John Neumann had stood only moments before.

"Thanks be to God," John said. "I could have been killed by that mast!" He knelt down on the wet deck and prayed. "God has saved my life," he thought to himself. "Surely this means that God wants me to go to America."

A few days later, the clipper ship sailed
into New York harbor. When John stepped ashore,
he felt lost. New York was a very busy city.
All day John walked up and down the streets of
New York.

He was looking for a priest he could talk to.
But no churches were open. By the end
of the day, John was hungry and tired. At last he
decided to rent a room for the night. The next
day he would try again.

The innkeeper was a kind woman. She fixed
John a hot drink and some bread. Then she said,
"You say you are from Bohemia? That is a long
way away. What brings you to America?"

John was grateful for the food and the chance
to talk with someone. He told the innkeeper the
whole story of how he decided to come to America.

"I want to be a pastor," said John. "I want to help the German settlers. I want to tell them about God's love." Then John explained, "Many German settlers in America do not speak English. When they go to church on Sunday, they do not understand what their pastor is saying. If I can preach to them in their own language, they will feel more at home in the church."

"How did you find out that the German settlers needed a pastor?" asked the innkeeper.

"I read in a newspaper that America needs priests who speak German," John answered. "I think that was God's way of telling me to come here."

"Do you know anyone here?"

"No," said John. "But I've been looking for a church where the pastor speaks German. He will tell me where I am needed."

The innkeeper looked doubtful. She lit a candle to show John up the steps to his room. All the way up, she shook her head. "Seems foolish to me," she said. "New York is so big. What if you do not find a German-speaking priest? What if there is no job for you here?"

"It may sound foolish," John admitted as he said good night. "But I know that God wants me to be here. I know he will help me."

The next day, John began looking again.
He stopped everyone he met as he walked along the
bustling New York streets. He asked if anyone knew
a priest who spoke German. But his English was
so poor that some people could not understand him.
Others pushed him aside and muttered at him.

But John kept asking and asking. Finally, someone told him to go to Father Raffeiner at Saint Nicholas Church on Second Street.

John had a happy surprise when he found the church. Father Raffeiner spoke German!

"Willkommen!" (That means "welcome" in German.) "Willkommen!" shouted Father Raffeiner when John arrived. He gave John a big hug. "Of course we need pastors," he said when he heard John's story. "God be praised for sending you to us."

All day Father Raffeiner and John Neumann
talked about the German settlers who had come
to America. Many of them lived in New York City.
Father Raffeiner spoke German to them each Sunday.
But many others lived in the forests and on the
farms of western New York. No one ever told
them stories about Jesus. No one ever gave them
Holy Communion. Here was a job for John Neumann.
Here was the reason he had come to America.
He would go to Williamsville and be pastor to the
settlers there.

One bright June day, John boarded a canal boat for the next part of his trip. After a while, a woman sat down beside him. She spoke German, too, so they talked together. "There is something I must tell you," she said sadly. "Many people don't like the German settlers. They think that we talk funny."

"I don't mind if people laugh at me,"
answered John.

"But they do more than laugh," said the woman.
"Sometimes they say mean things. And sometimes
they try to hurt us."

During the next few days on the boat, John thought about what the woman had told him. But he always remembered his decision. He had come to help the settlers. He would help them no matter what happened.

When John got off the canal boat, he traveled by horse and wagon to Williamsville. Williamsville was a very small town. It had just four houses. And its little stone church was not finished. The church had no roof. But John did not mind. He was eager for his real work in America to begin.

On John's first Sunday in Williamsville,
German settlers came from several miles away to
worship. They were very, very happy. For the
first time in many months they would hear their
pastor speak to them in German. Father John told
them about God's love. He told them beautiful
stories about Jesus.

Suddenly, something landed on the church floor.
"Thump. Thud." All the people looked up.
Someone was throwing rocks over the wall.

John ducked as a rock landed near the
altar where he stood. The settlers looked around.
They were frightened.

"What is happening?" cried one of the children.
"It's all right, little one," comforted Father John.
"Some people don't like us Germans. They want us to go back home across the ocean."

He bent down and took the little boy on his knee.
John patted the boy's head and dried his tears.
Then he looked at the people gathered in his church.

"Don't show your fear," he advised. "Then the people who are throwing the rocks will go away and leave us alone."

So John continued the Sunday worship service. The people sang hymns and praised God. Finally, the thudding and thumping stopped. No more rocks were thrown. (And no one ever threw rocks at the church again.)

John could see now that the German settlers really needed him. He thanked God for helping him come to America. No matter how lonely he was in this new land, he would help the settlers. So John visited the settlers when they were sick. He taught them. He showed them that God loved them. And always he carried pretty pictures and candy with him for the children.

A Biographical Sketch of John Neumann

Born in 1811 in Prachatitz, Czechoslovakia, John Neumann spent his adult life serving German immigrants in the United States. While in the seminary in Budweis, John read reports of the Leopoldine Society calling for missionaries to work in America. He felt called to go there.

With little money and no security that a position awaited him in the United States, John sailed from Le Havre on April 11, 1836. He arrived in New York forty days later. Ordained as a priest in June, John was immediately sent out to the Niagara Frontier. There, he ministered to the German settlers in the territory around Buffalo — an area of nine hundred square miles. After four years, however, John realized that he could no longer endure the loneliness of the frontier. He needed fellowship.

So, in 1840, John joined the Redemptorist Fathers in Pittsburgh. Soon he became head of the Redemptorists in America. Then, in 1852, he was appointed the Bishop of Philadelphia. During the eight years before his death, John built a cathedral and eighty churches and organized the first Catholic school system in the United States.

Despite this great burst of activity, John Neumann was a quiet man. And it was his quietness which children responded to. A common sight on the streets of Philadelphia was of the Roman Catholic bishop giving out candy and brightly-colored pictures to the children who surged happily around him.

In 1860 John Neumann died. He left behind the memory of a quiet man who joyfully responded to God's call to serve others. Often lonely, an immigrant in a strange land, John devoted himself and his considerable talents to the German settlers both in New York and Pennsylvania who longed for a word of the old language and a remembrance of home. His presence in America seemed to bring Christ closer.

It was this joyful devotion to God and humanity which prompted the Roman Catholic Church, in 1977, to declare John Neumann a saint.